Wishing you a

Merry Christmas

and peace throughout the year.

Engage Books

Christmas Coloring Card
Christmas Cookies
120 total pages
A5 (5.83 x 8.27)

Design © 2021 Engage Books (Activities)

All rights reserved. No part of this book may be stored in a retrieval system, reproduced or transmitted in any form or by any other means without written permission from the publisher or a licence from the Canadian Copyright Licensing Agency.

Engage Books

Mailing address:
Blank Classic
PO BOX 4608
Main Station Terminal
349 West Georgia Street
Vancouver, BC
Canada, V6B 4A1

Cover design by: Lauren Dick

ISBN: 978-1-77476-643-9

FIRST EDITION / FIRST PRINTING

peace
&
joy

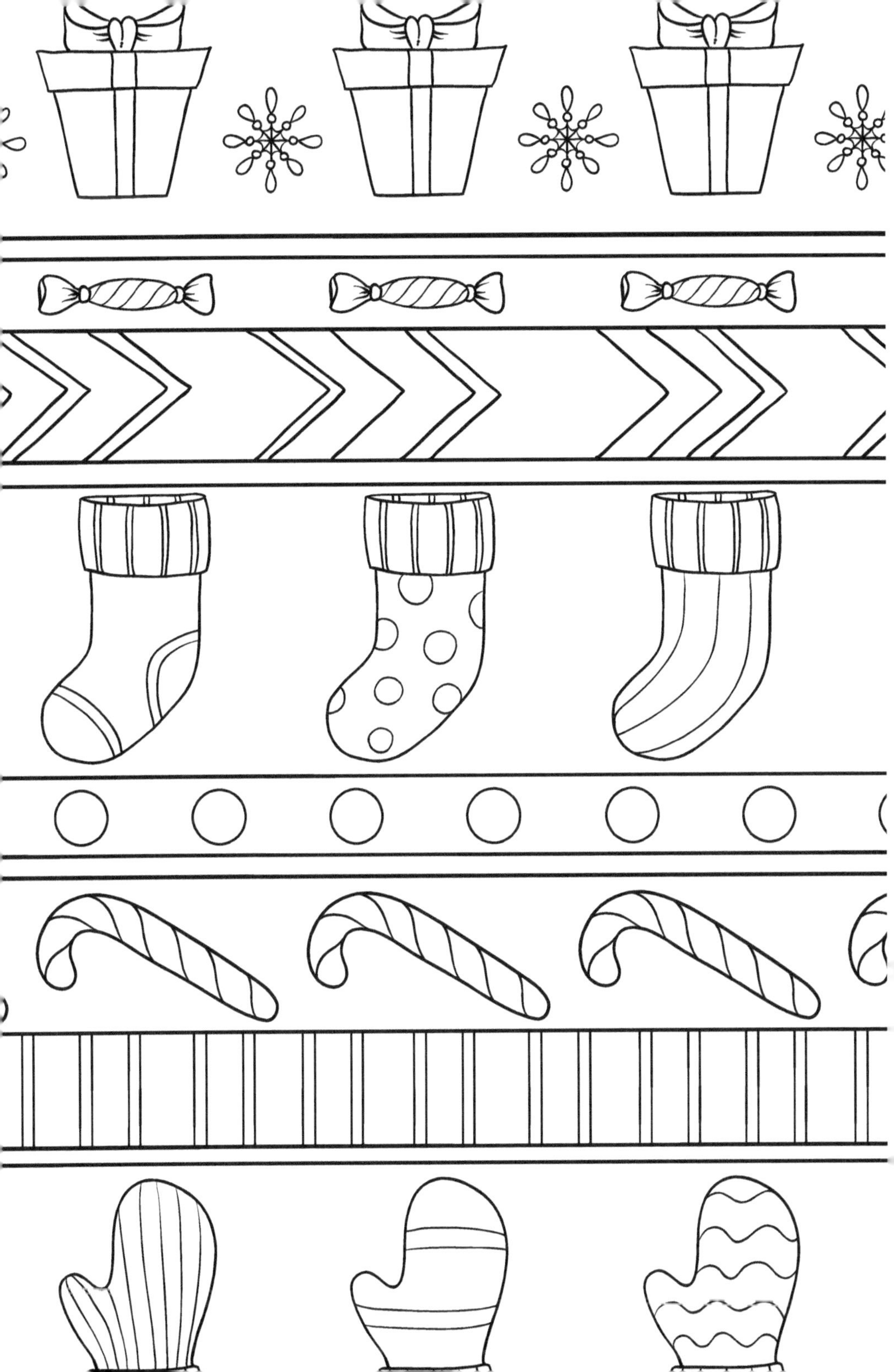

www.ingramcontent.com/pod-product-compliance
Lightning Source LLC
Chambersburg PA
CBHW050010070726
47598CB00014B/549